Carlo Pietrangeli and Fabrizio Mancinelli

THE VATICAN
City and Gardens

MONUMENTI, MUSEI E GALLERIE PONTIFICIE

1

CONTENTS

Cover: the dome of St. Peter's seen from the Vatican Gardens.

Inside front cover: the Sacristy of St. Peter's in the late eighteenth century. Fresco in the circular room of the Etruscan Museum.

Title page: the coat-of-arms of Pope John Paul II in front of the Palace of the Government.

Page 64: the rose bower in the Vatican Gardens.

Inside back cover: the coats-of-arms of the popes.

Back cover: the bronze entrance door to the Apostolic Palaces, defended by the Swiss Guards.

1. Vatican City. To the right (north) of the basilica are the Sistine Chapel and the Apostolic Palaces; further north, the vast complex of the Library and the Vatican Museums; above, in the Gardens, the Palazzina of Leo XIII with the Radio Tower.

2. Vatican City. Below left (north) are the Vatican Museums, with the museum housing the collections formerly in the Lateran and the Pinacoteca in the foreground; further up, the Courtyard of the Pigna, the Library and the Belvedere Courtyards. At the center the basilica and St. Peter's Square with the Apostolic Palaces. To the right the Vatican Gardens.

Texts by Fabrizio Mancinelli (Vatican City, St. Peter's, Apostolic Palaces and Vatican Museums) and Carlo Pietrangeli (Vatican Gardens); botanical consultant: Anna Lucia Francesconi.
© Copyright 1985 by SCALA, Istituto Fotografico Editoriale, Antella, Florence
Editors: Daniele Casalino, Karin Stephan
Layout: Fried Rosenstock
Photographs: SCALA, except inside front cover and nos. 32, 49, 80 (Vatican Museums); nos. 25, 26, 33, 89, 113 (Mario Carrieri, Rome); nos. 1, 71 (Pubbliaerfoto, Milan); no. 2 (F. Quilici, Rome); no. 42 (Lichtbildwerkstätte "Alpenland", Vienna); no. 10 (Alinari, Florence); no. 52 (Kupferstichkabinett, Berlin)
Printed in Italy by Sogema Marzari Spa, Schio 1985

2

2

The Vatican City

The Vatican City stands near the right bank of the Tiber on high ground which once formed the ancient *ager Vaticanus*. The Emperor Caligula (37-41 A.D.) built a Circus there, to the left of where the basilica of St. Peter's now stands, and placed in it the Egyptian obelisk now in the centre of the square. Nero (54-68 A.D.) enlarged the Circus and it was there and in the neighbouring gardens that he had the first Christian martyrs tortured, in 64 A.D. Among those martyred was St. Peter. To the north of the Circus and separated from it by a road, there was a slope, and on the top of the slope a necropolis, which was even at that time ancient. Here the prince of the apostles was buried. Over his tomb the Emperor Constantine (306-337) erected after 324, probably in 330, a majestic basilica; the present basilica was built, between the fifteenth and seventeenth centuries, as a replacement of the earlier one. During the Middle Ages a few buildings were constructed next to the basilica, but the popes only resided in them temporarily and usually because of an unstable political situation, which had forced them to withdraw from their normal residence, the Lateran. In the ninth century, Leo IV built a circle

of walls around the area, until that time in open countryside, transforming the Vatican into a secure fortified citadel. In the thirteenth century, Nicholas III, who lived permanently in the Vatican, built the first real pontifical palace. This palace-cum-fortress, built on a rectangular plan, probably had defense towers at each corner. It was built around a courtyard, known today as the Courtyard of the Pappagallo, and incorporated to the south a fortified construction built by Innocent III north of the basilica. In 1377, after the return of Gregory XI from his exile in Avignon, the Vatican became the permanent residence of the popes and, in the following century with Nicholas V, a very grand programme of renovation was begun. The Apostolic Palace was modified and Nicholas V completed the north wing; to him we also owe the project for the enlargement of St. Peter's. Sixtus IV is responsible for the Sistine Chapel and the definitive arrangement of the Vatican Library, already begun by Nicholas V. During the papacy of Innocent VIII a summer residence, the Palazzetto del Belvedere, was built on the hill north of the palace. During the last decade of the fifteenth century, Alexander VI Borgia had the Borgia Tower built

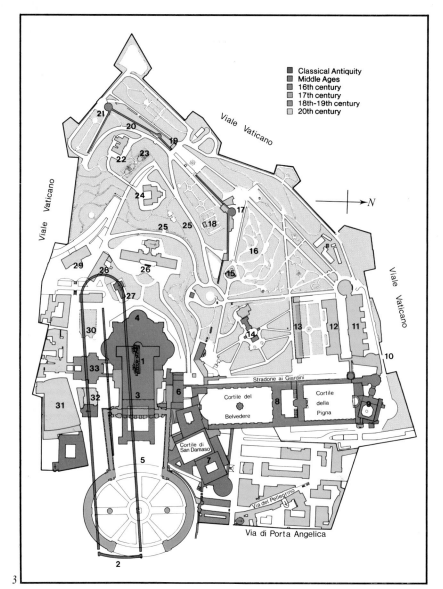

and also had the apartment on the first floor of the north wing of the palace decorated by Pinturicchio.

With Julius II, the original complex of the Apostolic Palace was given, through the work of Bramante, a renaissance appearance. The architect planned to connect the Apostolic Palace to the Palazzetto del Belvedere with a grandiose courtyard, the Belvedere Courtyard. He also altered the plan of the palace on the side facing Rome: he hid the medieval facade built by Nicholas III with three rows of loggias. Also drawn up by Bramante was the first real project for the reconstruction of St. Peter's. Among the works of decoration commissioned by Julius II are the ceiling of the Sistine Chapel, painted by Michelangelo, and the frescoes in the pope's own apartments, on the second floor of the north wing of the palace, by Raphael. Leo X, his successor, also entrusted to Raphael the decoration of Bramante's Loggias.

With Paul III, Antonio da Sangallo was given the task of remodernizing the south wing of the old palace, to be used for public ceremonies. Paul III also commissioned the Last Judgement in the Sistine Chapel from Michelangelo, ordering that this fresco should have precedence over the reconstruction of St. Peter's. During the second half of the sixteenth century, under Pius IV, the west wing and the north facade of the Belvedere Courtyard, with the famous Nicchione, were completed. The architect of these plans was Pirro Ligorio, from whom the pope also commissioned the Casina, an important example of mannerist architecture, which today houses the Papal Academy of Science. Gregory XIII had the palace on the north side of the Courtyard of St. Damasus built; the facade of this building is a continuation of Bramante's Loggias. This pope also commissioned from Ottaviano Mascherino the construction of the Gallery of Maps and the Tower of Winds above it, the first Vatican observatory. Sixtus V entrusted to Domenico Fontana the building of the

4. *The Hall of Papal Audiences and the Sacristy of St. Peter's.*

5. *Palazzo del Tribunale, the Mosaic School and the Railway Station (to the left), the church of Santo Stefano degli Abissini (below, center), the Palace of the Government (to the right), the Ethiopian College (above, right) and the Palazzina Marconi (above, center).*

6. *The Vatican Radio Tower with the Palazzina of Leo XIII, now the headquarters of the Vatican Radio, the residence of the director of the Vatican Radio, the Fontana dell'Aquilone, the Gardener's House (below, center).*

7. *The Science Academy with the Casina of Pius IV (center) and the Pinacoteca (above).*

new Apostolic Palace, which to this day is the residence of the popes, closing in on the east side the Courtyard of St. Damasus. Also to Domenico Fontana we owe the new building of the Vatican Library where the Salone Sistino now is and which cuts across the Belvedere Courtyard.

In the seventeenth century, during the papacy of Paul V, the construction of St. Peter's was completed. This pope also commissioned the building under which the Stradone ai Giardini, which leads to the museums, passes; he endowed the palace with a monumental entrance, of which the Bronze Door still stands, and embellished the gardens with many fountains. Alexander VII entrusted to Gian Lorenzo Bernini the building of the colonnade of St. Peter's Square and the Scala Regia. With Benedict XIV the history of the museums begins: in 1756 he founded the Sacred Museum of the Vatican Library. In 1767, Clement XIII founded the Profane Museum of the Vatican Library. Under the auspices of Clement XIV and Pius VI, the architects Michelangelo Simonetti and Giuseppe Camporese built the Pio-Clementine Museum, transforming completely the Palazzetto del Belvedere. In the following century, Pius VII commissioned Pasquale Belli to build the Braccio Nuovo, on a project by Raffaello Stern.

During this century, with Pius XI, a new construction programme was begun, in part due to the new status of the Vatican after the 1929 treaty, which resolved the complex controversy between the Holy See and Italy which had arisen after the conquest of Rome (1870). In 1931 Guglielmo Marconi set up the Vatican Radio, and in 1929 Luca Beltrami built the Pinacoteca. Also new buildings for the administration of the new state were built, including the Palace of the Government, by Giuseppe Momo. To John XXIII and Paul VI we owe the building which houses the collections formerly in the Lateran and the Hall of Papal Audiences.

8

St. Peter's

The facade of St. Peter's was built by Carlo Maderno between 1608 and 1612, during the papacy of Paul V, but remained without the planned bell-towers; these were designed to draw attention to the cupola and thus to lighten somewhat the effect of the whole. Gian Lorenzo Bernini put forward his solution of the problem in 1637: twin bell-towers with columns at each corner and crowned by spires, each one in all 100 metres high. During the construction of the left tower, subsidence occurred in the portico and the project was therefore abandoned. With Innocent X, the successor of Urban VIII, Bernini fell into disgrace and the bell-tower was removed. But, after the death of Innocent X in 1655, Alexander VII recalled the artist and entrusted him with the task of transforming the square facing the basilica into a huge atrium, with the obelisk from Caligula's Circus in the middle. Some of the work had in fact already been done by Domenico Fontana as early as 1586. On 28 August 1656 the pope placed the first stone; 140 statues of saints crown the work which was completed in a decade. The huge ellyptical semicircular square was built originally to face the church rather than the city. At the end of the two arms of colonnades, a central sector was designed to leave open two side entrances. The two straight wings that join the colonnades to the church have the function of making the church seem closer to the square than it is.

The dynamic effect of church and square was considerably changed by the construction of Via della Conciliazione. The demolition in 1937 of the Spina quarter, so called because of its peculiar shape, has in fact inverted the effect envisaged by Bernini.

The basilica of St. Peter's stands on the slopes of the hill of the Vatican, on the site of the basilica built by Constantine and of the apostle's tomb. He was buried *in humili sepultura*, in a ditch hollowed in the bare earth and covered by a few tiles, not far from the place of his martyrdom, in a pagan cemetery. In the second century a monument was built on the place: two niches were placed over one another, against a wall. Constantine's architects built the basilica with five naves, aligning it with the monument, over the pagan necropolis, which was partially razed and filled with débris to create a level surface. In front of the facade, which was decorated with mosaics, there was a courtyard surrounded by colonnades, in the centre of which Pope Symmachus in the sixth century built a basin for ablutions, and the

9

10

8. *St. Peter's Square. Christmas blessing "Urbi et Orbi".*

9. *St. Peter's Square, Via della Conciliazione, Castel Sant'Angelo and the Tiber, seen from the dome of the basilica.*

10. *St. Peter's Square and the Borghi before the demolition of the Spina (1937).*

11

stone pine cone, now in the Courtyard of the Pigna. The apostle's monument was left visible at the centre of the transept and the papal altar was built over it; its lower niche corresponds today to the niche for the consecration of the episcopal robes. The mosaic of Christ, which has been much restored, was made after Leo III. The figures of St. Peter and St. Paul are of the time of Urban VIII. The casket for the robes is of the time of Benedict XIV. Above the niche is a grille with an inscription of Innocent III.

The place nearest to the tomb of St. Peter is the chapel of the same name, also known as the Clementine Chapel, because it was restored under Clement VIII. The chapel dates from the time of Gregory I.

During the Middle Ages Constantine's basilica underwent numerous changes and additions. But in the fifteenth century it was no longer big enough and, most important of all, its structure had become unsound. At first it was decided simply to enlarge the church, and in 1452 Bernardo Rossellino was entrusted with the work by Nicholas V. He drew up a plan for the transformation of the area of the presbytery; but the consequent work was interrupted by the death of the pope in 1455, when the walls were still less than two metres high. It was Julius II who decided to reconstruct the basilica completely. Donato Bramante was put in charge of the project; his conception was of a building in the form of a Greek cross framed by a square formed by four towers. There were to be four small cupolas and a large central one supported by a drum with windows; at the end of each arm of the cross there was

11. View of the apse and the transept.

12. The dome and the Tower of Winds (in the foreground), seen from the Nicchione della Pigna.

to be a projecting semicircular apse. On 18 April 1506 Julius II placed the first stone, at the foot of the pillar named after St. Veronica.

On the death of Bramante in 1514 only the central arches and four pillars had been completed. Leo X appointed Fra Giocondo da Verona and Giuliano da Sangallo to continue the work. On his death in 1515 Fra Giocondo was succeeded by Raphael, but the plan was changed: without destroying what Bramante had built they began to build a Latin cross. On the death of Raphael in 1520 the work was continued by his assistant Antonio da Sangallo and by Baldassarre Peruzzi. They returned to the Greek cross, but the work was interrupted again by the sack of Rome in 1527 and resumed under Paul III in 1534.

Antonio da Sangallo's wooden model of a building in the form of a Greek cross was accepted. In order to allow services to be held in the nave, he separated it from the building area by a wall. The alterations that Sangallo made to Bramante's design impeded the progress of the work until 1540.

When Sangallo died, Paul III transferred the task to Michelangelo. In 1547 he allowed Michelangelo the freedom to alter the design as he saw fit, and in 1549 he appointed him architect for life of the fabric of the church.

13

14

Michelangelo decided to return to Bramante's design, into which he introduced various changes made necessary, on the one hand by a different stylistic approach, and on the other by the need to give the whole structure a greater solidity. Despite continual difficulties, when Michelangelo died in 1564 the work was well in hand: the south transept was finished; the north transept and the drum for the cupola were almost finished. In 1564 Pius IV nominated Pirro Ligorio as chief architect of the fabric and Jacopo Vignola as second architect. But they were both opposed to Michelangelo's design, and were consequently dismissed in the following year. In 1567 Vignola was recalled. He died in 1573 and was replaced by Giacomo della Porta who in 1588, under Sixtus V, began to construct the cupola. In 1590 the task was completed, and Gregory XIV ordered work to begin on the construction of the cleristory. In the papacy of Clement VIII, the bronze sphere was put in position. Clement entrusted the decoration of the cupola in mosaic to Cavalier d'Arpino, who was assisted by Cesare Nebbia and Giovanni Vecchi, among others.

What survived of the old basilica (the nave and aisles) was structurally precarious, and in 1605, under Paul V, it began to be demolished. (The sepulchral monuments were preserved). The question now arose of whether to continue with Michelangelo's design or to draw up a new plan for the church in the form of a Latin cross; it was in order to decide this that the pope now invited the most famous architects of the day to present their designs. It was Carlo Maderno's design that was adopted, in the form of a Latin cross. The construction of the nave and aisles began on 8 March 1607. In 1612 the facade was complete, and in 1615 the whole church was finished and ready for the admiration of the faithful.

The problem remained of giving the required prominence to the tomb of St. Peter, which lay below the level of the new floor. (The new church was built on a higher level than Constantine's and, given the slope of the ground, on a higher level than

the remains, still visible, of the pagan necropolis within which the apostle was buried.) Urban VIII Barberini employed Bernini to build a canopy over the great altar. The work began on 19 June 1624. The bronze acquired from Livorno and from Venice proved to be insufficient, and so the artist suggested that the girders of the atrium and the ribbing of the cupola of the Pantheon be melted down. Hence the saying: "*Quod non fecerunt Barbari fecerunt Barberini*" (what the Barbarians left undone, was done by the Barberini). The quantity of bronze was such that, quite apart from the canopy, eighty cannons for the Castel Sant'Angelo were fashioned out of it. On 29 June 1633 the monument was consecrated. Four tendril-columns, on the model of those in Constantine's basilica, supported the canopy; they were decorated with bronze fringes and bronze tassels, and surmounted by four angels, by putti and by Barberini coats of arms. The casting was carried out by Gregorio de' Rossi under the direct supervision of Bernini; among Bernini's assistants was the young Francesco Borromini.

Among the works made by Bernini for St. Peter's is the magnificent reliquary in gilded bronze (the so-called throne of St. Peter, completed in the papacy of Alexander VII), a masterpiece of baroque art, which contains the wooden throne on which according to tradition, the apostle sat. In the "edifice" conceived by Bernini (and set up in the church in 1666) the reliquary is supported by St. Augustine, St. Ambrose, St. Athanasius and St. John Chrysostom, symbols of the eastern and western Churches as subject to Rome. A burst of sunlight with clouds and angels surrounds the window, and on the window is an image of the Holy Spirit.

The throne contained in the reliquary does not really belong to the first century A.D. The ivory decoration can be dated to the ninth century; it consists of a series of friezes with plant volutes, classical in origin, surrounding small figures of men, animals and mixtures of man and animal. At the centre of the back is the bust of an emperor, probably Charles the Bald (823-877). The panels on the front

13. *Domenico Tasselli: drawing reconstructing the portico and the facade of the old basilica (c. 1605).*

14. *School of Raphael: detail of a fresco in the Hall of Constantine, showing the interior of the old basilica (c. 1520).*

15. *The interior of the basilica.*

16. *The interior of the dome.*

16

11

17

17. *Gian Lorenzo Bernini: Apotheosis of the Holy Spirit.*

18. *Bronze statue of St. Peter enthroned, attributed to Arnolfo di Cambio.*

19. *Medieval papal throne, incorporated into the throne built by G. L. Bernini.*

20. *Antonio Averulino, called Filarete: the central door of St. Peter's, detail with St. Paul and St. Peter handing over the keys to Eugene IV.*

21. *Gian Lorenzo Bernini: monument to Urban VIII.*

22. *Michelangelo: Pietà.*

of the seat are an addition; they represent fantastic animals and the labours of Hercules; their date is disputed, but they are probably of the ninth century and contemporary with Lothar. Originally the throne was kept in the monastery of St. Martin, which stood where now stands the pillar named after St. Veronica.

The Pietà in St. Peter's is a youthful work of Michelangelo; he sculpted it between 1498 and 1500, for Cardinal Jean de Bilhères de Lagraulas, for the round Chapel of St. Petronilla in the old church of the Vatican. In the course of the centuries the Pietà was moved from one place to another. Finally, in 1749, Benedict XIV placed it where it is today, in the first chapel to the right of the entrance.

Antonio di Pietro Averulino (called "il Filarete") was summoned to Rome in 1433 to make the central bronze doors of St. Peter's – the first renaissance work in Rome. He was appointed to the task by Eugene IV Condulmer (1431-1447), who is represented next to St. Peter. The doors were placed in position on 14 August 1445; according to Giorgio Vasari the artist had worked on them for twelve years. Each door is decorated by three panels representing (on the left door) Christ enthroned, St. Paul, the condemnation and execution of St. Paul and his appearing to Plautilla; and on the right door the Virgin enthroned, St. Peter giving the keys to Eugene IV, the condemnation and crucifixion of St. Peter. The four horizontal reliefs illustrate events of the papacy of Eugene IV. The influence of antiquity is evident in the style as well as the iconography of the doors. Several elements (for example the figures of the two apostles) seem to be derived from palaeochristian art. The choice of themes represents the desire to celebrate the pope's attempts to achieve Christian unity. The two lower reliefs were added in 1620 by Paul V when the doors were incorporated in the new church; they had originally been made for Constantine's church.

18

19

20

21

22

23

The Apostolic Palaces and the Vatican Museums

The Courtyard of St. Damasus opens onto the south towards St. Peter's Square. It is formed by three distinct buildings: to the west is the oldest nucleus of the Apostolic Palaces with the Loggias of Donato Bramante; to the north the wing of Gregory XIII and to the east the Palace of Sixtus V, from which the pope appears on religious festivals to give his blessing. Before the work done by Bramante the Apostolic Palace was a collection of buildings of different periods built around the Courtyard of the Pappagallo. The south wing (which includes a building with a tower constructed by Innocent III), with the Sala Ducale and the Sala Regia, was constructed by Nicholas III, as was the east wing (which was later completed on the north side by Boniface VIII). Then there is the north wing, which was added by Nicholas V, with three towers at the corners (the north-west one was built by Alexander VI) and the Sistine Chapel, which had a defensive as well as a religious function. On the eastern facade, towards Rome, there were loggias even in the medieval building, and on the ground floor a portico. When Julius II had the Belvedere Courtyard built he decided to decorate this eastern facade in renaissance style. Bramante began the work in about 1508. He closed the portico on the ground floor and

replaced the two upper galleries with three rows of loggias, increasing thereby the height of the facade. A stairway on the south side with wide shallow steps (which in the nineteenth century Pius VII replaced with the ramp with landings and steps) joined Bramante's three Loggias. The work was finished by Raphael, who modified the project slightly by replacing the final loggia with a trabeated peristyle. The loggias of Gregory XIII, similar in every respect to Bramante's, are part of Gregory's Palace, and give onto the north side of the Courtyard of St. Damasus.

The Palace of Sixtus V, forming the east side of the Courtyard of St. Damasus, is the work of Domenico Fontana. It has a square plan with a rectangular courtyard in the middle, and to the north it joins the Palace of Gregory XIII. The facade giving onto the Courtyard of St. Damasus is an extension of the loggias; it had been begun by Martino Longhi, but was finished by Fontana.

On the second floor, in the Papal Suite (the "Appartamento Nobile Pontificio"), is the Clementine Hall (named after Clement VIII, who completed the construction begun by Sixtus V), possibly by Taddeo Landini. The room has a large "trompe l'œil" vault ceiling and frescoes by Giovanni and Cherubino Alberti and by Paul Bril. The Papal Suite was

25

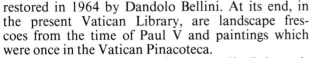
24

23. The Courtyard of St. Damasus with Bramante's Loggias (to the left).

24. Palace of Sixtus V. Sunday blessing from the pope's private apartments.

25. St. Peter's Square seen from the window of the pope's private apartments, with the faithful awaiting the Sunday blessing.

26. The Scala Regia, towards the Bronze Door.

26

restored in 1964 by Dandolo Bellini. At its end, in the present Vatican Library, are landscape frescoes from the time of Paul V and paintings which were once in the Vatican Pinacoteca.

The main entrance to the Apostolic Palaces is through the Bronze Door, built in 1618 on a commission by Paul V, as is recorded in an inscription. The door is all that is left of the elaborate entrance built by Martino Ferrabosco and Jan van Xanten, later replaced by Bernini's Portico of Constantine (the long rectangular building on the right side of the basilica). At the end of this is the access to the

28

27. Gian Lorenzo Bernini: the first flight of the Scala Regia and the equestrian statue of Constantine.

28. Sala Ducale. In the foreground the "aula tertia," then the "aula secunda" and, in the background, the entrance to the Sala Regia.

Scala Regia, with thirteen steps and a grand ser- liana crowned by two winged representations of Fame, holding the coat of arms of Alexander VII. On the right is the equestrian statue of Constantine, built by Bernini on a commission from Innocent X and, on the left, the entrance to the atrium of St. Peter's. The stairway connects the portico and the atrium to the Sala Regia; Antonio da Sangallo had built a stairway here earlier, but it was narrow, bare and badly lit. Alexander VII charged Bernini with the task of renovating it completely and this was put into effect between 1664 and 1666. The stairway is divided by a landing into two flights. The first is lined, so to speak, with an internal colon- nade of Ionic style, supporting on its architrave a barrel-vault, which also serves the purpose of mak- ing the construction more solid. The effect in per- spective which is caused by the progressive lower- ing of the height of the vault, of the columns and also the narrowing of the width of the columns, al- lowed Bernini to camouflage the irregular, trape- zoid, shape of the unit. The effect of perspective is emphasized by the light which falls almost entirely on the landing at the end of the first flight. The se- cond flight is, on the other hand, only an adaptation of the stairway by Sangallo. Next to the Scala Re- gia, is the Scala dei Morti (the stairway of the dead), which derives its name from the fact that it is used for carrying the bodies of the popes into St. Peter's.

From the Sala Regia, *aula magna vel prima*, one passes into the Sala Ducale, which comprises both the *aula secunda* and *tertia* (the latter, in the build- ing of Innocent III, is the oldest part of the palaces); the present room is, in fact, the result of the union of two rooms, which in the medieval building were totally separate units. In the *aula tertia* the public

29. *The pope's Library in the Papal Suite.*

30. *The Niccoline Chapel with the frescoes showing episodes from the lives of Saints Stephen and Lawrence.*

consistory was held by the popes when they officially received those sovereign princes, or dukes, which in the Roman ceremonial are called the dukes of major power: hence the name of the room. In the sixteenth century, under Clement VII, the ceilings of the two rooms were lowered and covered with vaults and lunettes by Antonio da Sangallo. The work was continued by Paul III, and the decoration begun by Paul IV and finished by Gregory XIII. It is difficult to name with any certainty the artists who decorated the two rooms with grotesques, landscapes and stories. One scholar maintains that the landscapes in the frieze in the *aula tertia* are by Giovanni da Udine; the grotesques in the lunettes in the same room, on the south wall, are by Matteino da Siena, while the landscapes on the north wall were painted in this century, in the time of Benedict XV, and cover four little windows where once the ladies could watch the ceremony, on Holy Thursday, when the pope washed the feet of twelve poor priests dressed as apostles. In the seventeenth century, the two rooms were converted into a single one by Bernini on a commission from Alexander VII. The two rooms were not symmetrical and their shape was not regular, because the old medieval building had followed the shape of the neighbouring hillside. Bernini solved this problem by giving the opening between the two rooms an amusing curtain held up by two winged putti; the effect of this perspective correction is now partly lost, due to the geometrical designs on the marble floor, which replaced, under Benedict XV, the old tiles.

Fra Giovanni da Fiesole, called Beato Angelico, decorated the *cappella parva superior* in the tower of Innocent III on a commission by Nicholas V. This chapel is today known as the Niccoline Chapel. Angelico also frescoed the Studiolo of Nicholas V, between 1447 and 1449 and again between 1451 and 1454, about which we know very little. Between 1452 and 1455 he also frescoed the Chapel of St. Nicholas, next to the Sala Regia, which was later destroyed by Antonio da Sangallo in order to make room for the Scala del Maresciallo, then the main entrance to the Apostolic Palaces. Angelico had painted for Eugene IV, who had originally called him to Rome, another chapel in St. Peter's probably between 1445 and 1449, but nothing is left of that. The Niccoline Chapel was painted between 1448 and 1451 and the two rows of frescoes depict stories from the lives of St. Stephen and St. Lawrence. The pope in these frescoes has the features of Nicholas V. In the corners the Doctors of the Church are portrayed, and on the ceiling are the four evangelists. As was usual in the fifteenth century, Angelico was most probably helped a great deal by apprentices and collaborators, among whom Benozzo Gozzoli, but the majority of the scenes were painted entirely by himself.

The Borgia Tower and Apartment date from the time of Alexander VI Borgia. This apartment, where the pope lived and died, occupies two rooms in the tower (the Halls of the Creed and of the Sibyls), the following three rooms (the Halls of the Mysteries, of the Saints and of the Liberal Arts), the Hall of the

31

Popes in the northern wing, and a group of small rooms which can be reached through the Hall of the Liberal Arts in the west wing. The Hall of the Popes was used by the pope for official functions, while the Hall of the Liberal Arts served as his private study. Bernardino Betti, called Pinturicchio, was entrusted with the decoration of these rooms; in 1492 he left Orvieto, where he was working in the Cathedral, and by 1494 had finished this work. The Hall of the Popes was not included in this decoration, and its ceiling was frescoed by Perin del Vaga and Giovanni da Udine, in the time of Leo X. In the Hall of the Mysteries of the Faith are depicted scenes from the incarnation and the resurrection of Christ. In the Hall of the Saints, there are scenes from the life of the Virgin and St. Sebastian, of Susanna, of St. Barbara, of St. Catherine of Alexandria and of St. Anthony Abbot and St. Paul Hermit. On the ceiling is the myth of Isis and Osiris and the bull Apis. In the Hall of the Liberal Arts are the allegories of the Trivium and the Quadrivium; in the Hall of the Creed, prophets and apostles; in the Hall of the Sibyls, prophets and sibyls. In this apartment today are exhibited the works of the Collection of Modern Religious Art, opened in 1973 by Paul VI, which includes works given to the pope

31. The Hall of the Saints in the Borgia Apartment (which today houses the Collection of Modern Religious Art).

32. The Borgia Tower seen from the courtyard of the same name.

33. The Courtyard of the Parrot, looking towards the Borgia Courtyard.

34. The Courtyard of the Parrot, looking towards the Courtyard of St. Damasus.

by artists and collectors of our time.

Both Alexander VI's predecessor and his successor were members of the della Rovere family: Sixtus IV (1471-1484) and Julius II (1503-1513), both portrayed, the former as pope and the latter as cardinal, in the fresco of the Nomination of Bartolomeo Platina, in 1475, as prefect of the Vatican Library. Today this fresco is in the Pinacoteca, but it was intended as decoration for one of the halls which Sixtus IV had set

32

33

34

35. The Sistine Chapel, seen from the Vatican Gardens.

36. The Sistine Chapel.

aside to house the public library. This had been a project of Nicholas V, but was only realized by Sixtus IV. The rooms on the ground floor of the north wing of the Apostolic Palaces, below what was to become the Borgia Apartment, were used for this purpose. The first of these rooms housed the Latin Library and the second the Greek. These were followed by the Secret Library, with a collection of the most precious manuscripts, and the Pontifical Library, which held the papal archives and registers. Domenico and Davide del Ghirlandaio decorated the lunettes in the Latin Library with portrayals of the Fathers of the Church and classical philosophers, and Melozzo da Forlì painted the scene of the investiture of Platina on the wall between the two windows in this same room. In the Greek Library, the decoration consists in a row of corinthian columns on the walls, and two portraits in the lunettes, perhaps teacher and disciple; but there is nothing left of the decoration of the next two rooms. A recent restoration has brought to the light the decoration on the ceiling of the Pontifical Library: an intricate, but stylized, floral decoration, in chiaroscuro, grey on a white background.

At the same time as he was creating the first library. Sixtus IV had the Palatine Chapel built, (1475-1483), later called the Sistine Chapel, by Giovannino de' Dolci, after a project by Baccio Pontelli.

The Sistine Chapel was built between 1475 and 1480, and by 1483 even the decoration on the walls was complete. Perugino was entrusted with its decoration; he began with the wall behind the altar, and also painted the now lost Annunciation. In 1481 he was joined by Sandro Botticelli, Domenico del Ghirlandaio and Cosimo Rosselli and the following year by Luca Signorelli, who completed the work. The frescoes are on three levels: on the first, painted tapestries, on the second, stories from the lives of Christ and Moses, and above this, the series of portraits of the popes.

36

37

The three popes (1484-1503) who succeeded Sixtus IV did not make any alteration to the chapel; but Julius II decided to have the ceiling frescoed by Michelangelo. The artist did not receive the order with any great pleasure, but nonetheless began work in May 1508. By september 1510 half the work was finished, and, on 14 August 1511, the pope insisted that it should be unveiled. By October of the following year, the work was finished and on the day of All Saints, Julius II inaugurated it with a solemn mass.

The initial plan had consisted in twelve enormous figures of the apostles, but the artist had rejected this plan as unworthy. Given complete freedom of action, Michelangelo proceeded to create a monumental painted architectural structure, covering the real ceiling, but without any *trompe l'œil* intentions. In the nine large spaces thus created, he painted episodes from Genesis, from the creation to the drunkenness of Noah. In the corners of each scene are *Ignudi*, and in the spaces between the side lunettes seven prophets alternate with five sibyls. In the four corners of the ceiling, he painted the stories of David and Goliath, of Judith and Holofernes, the punishment of Aman and the bronze serpent. In the lunettes above, are the ancestors of Christ, melancholy figures in expectation of the Messiah. Throughout this monumental task Michelangelo refused any help and worked entirely alone.

Twenty-one years later, in 1533, Clement VII called Michelangelo back to Rome to paint the Last Judgement on the wall behind the altar, and, in 1534, Paul III confirmed this commission. Once again the artist was very reluctant about the commission and waited two years before beginning the work. In order to make space for Michelangelo's fresco, Perugino's work had to be destroyed. On 31 October 1541, the scaffolding was removed and Paul III celebrated vespers beneath the monumental work, which filled Rome with "wonder and amazement." The unusual location of this subject matter had been suggested by Clement VII, who had wished to commemorate in this way the tragic events of the year 1527, the sack of Rome.

When Julius II became pope in 1503, he was very unwilling to occupy the Borgia Apartment and, in 1507, moved to the floor above. The Sala Vecchia degli Svizzeri was the entrance to the new apartment, the Room of the Chiaroscuri was the first antechamber, from which one passed into the pope's *cubiculum* and to the *stufetta*, the bathroom. The actual apartment consisted in the Hall of Constantine and the three following rooms; the Hall of Constantine was used for official ceremonies, the Room of Heliodorus served as a secret ante-room, the Stanza della Segnatura was a private library, and the Room of the Fire in the Borgo was the usual dining

37. Michelangelo: frescoes on the ceiling of the Sistine Chapel.

38. Raphael: The School of Athens, in the Stanza della Segnatura.

room. Julius II ordered Raphael to decorate these rooms, destroying the previous decorations, among which, alas, a fresco by Piero della Francesca. Raphael frescoed the Stanza della Segnatura between 1508 and 1511 choosing as subject matter, probably on the pope's suggestion, the apotheosis of the supreme ideas: of revealed Truth (Disputation of the Sacrament), of rational Truth (School of Athens), of Beauty (Parnassus), and of the Good (portrayed by Virtue and the Law). In the Room of Heliodorus, painted between 1511 and 1514, he represented Providence protecting the Church. In the Room of the Fire in the Borgo (1514-1517), for the most part painted by apprentices, there are a series of episodes illustrating popes who chose the name Leo, in homage

to Leo X, who had become pope on the death of Julius II, in 1514. For the Hall of Constantine, Raphael prepared a few drawings, but the actual decoration of the room is due to Giulio Romano and Giovanni Francesco Penni, who worked on it between 1517 and 1524.

Raphael worked on the Loggias both as painter and architect. He completed Bramante's project which, at the time of Leo X, stopped at the second loggia; Raphael added the third in order to complete the succession of the classical styles, each one on a different level. The project was begun in 1517 and completed in 1519. Raphael began on the second loggia, but never actually worked on the project himself, simply handing over drawings to his workshop, which included Giovanni da Udine, Giulio Romano, G. Francesco Penni, Perin del Vaga, and others of lesser renown. The decoration was for the most part derived from classical art, of which there were many examples in Rome, such as the *Domus Aurea*. Giovanni da Udine in particular examined them with great care, attempting to reproduce them exactly even from the point of view of technique. In each vaulted ceiling classical and profane themes surround four scenes from the Old and New Testa-

ments. In all there are fifty-two scenes, only four of which from the Gospels, which are known as Raphael's Bible. This loggia was used by Leo X as his own private museum, where he placed numerous classical statues in the niches between the windows.

Giovanni da Udine also worked on the first loggia, which he finished after 1519. He painted on its ceilings "pergolas with vines heavy with bunches of grapes, with jasmine, with roses and various kinds of animals and birds" (Vasari). Then, between 1560 and 1564, he decorated the third loggia, known as the Cosmographical Loggia, with grotesques, and allegorical stucco work.

39. Bramante's second Loggia, called Raphael's Loggia because Raphael was responsible for the frescoes.

40. Bramante's first Loggia, called Giovanni da Udine's Loggia for the same reason.

41. Bramante's third Loggia, called the Cosmographical Loggia from the subject of the frescoes.

42. Marten van Heemskerck: Bramante's Loggias (detail of a drawing dating from 1533).

43. Bramante's Loggias.

44

The Belvedere Courtyard was designed by Bramante in order to provide an easy access from the Apostolic Palace to the Palazzetto del Belvedere of Innocent VIII, which was on a higher level on the *mons sancti Aegidii.* The space between the two, a large area surrounded by walls cultivated with vineyards and vegetable gardens, was difficult and uncomfortable to cross. Bramante planned to connect the two buildings with two long, parallel corridors, with many levels, topped by a terrace, almost like a raised road, which would have connected the second loggia of the Apostolic Palace to the first floor of the Belvedere. This terrace was to have been intended for horses as well. The highest covered gallery, which still stands today, connected the first loggia of the palace to the Courtyard of the Oranges, today the Octagonal Courtyard. The lower galleries were shorter, because the Belvedere Courtyard was on three different levels, which compensated for the different height of the two buildings. The connection between these different levels was through monumental staircases, of which few traces remain today. The construction of the library of Sixtus V and, much later, of the Braccio Nuovo, at the end of the middle level, involved the demolition of these staircases and the division of the original courtyard into the three present ones, the Belvedere Courtyard, the Library Courtyard and the Courtyard of the Pigna. On the low-

44. View of the Apostolic Palaces and the Vatican Museums from the dome of St. Peter's. In the foreground, the Sistine Chapel and the Borgia Tower; above, left, the Belvedere Courtyard, the Library Courtyard and the Courtyard of the Pigna; to the right, the Apostolic Palaces built around the Courtyards of the Parrot and of St. Damasus.

45. Gallery of Maps.

er level jousts, games and plays took place, which the public watched from the windows of the palace or from the steps of the staircase which led to the middle level. This was kept as a garden, like the upper one, which ended with a facade with an exedra at the centre and corinthian columns alternating with niches. The exedra did not cover the upper part of the Palazzetto del Belvedere which could be reached by a staircase of sixteen steps, eight concave and eight convex. The side galleries opened out like a portico on the upper and lower levels. The lower one was, however, closed and modified by Antonio da Sangallo under Paul III for reasons of stability. Bramante, who began the work in 1504, only partially completed the project, having laid only the foundations for the entire west wing. The work was continued by Raphael, An-

tonio da Sangallo, and later by Pirro Ligorio who, under Pius IV, completed the project with substantial modifications, such as the construction of the Nicchione, which replaced the exedra by Bramante.

The Gallery of Maps takes its name from the maps of the regions of Italy which were painted on its walls following the orders of Pope Gregory XIII in 1580. The dominican Ignazio Danti, a cosmographer, supplied the cartoons. It is in the west wing of the Belvedere Courtyard, above the corridor which contains the collections of the Vatican Library, on the same level as Raphael's Stanze. The task of building it was entrusted to the architect Ottaviano Mascherino probably around 1578. The gallery is 120 metres long and 6 wide; on the walls are rectangular windows and the ceiling is barrel-vaulted. At the centre of the wall on the courtyard side is an elegant "serliana" which opens onto a balcony. The attic above dates from the time of Urban VIII. Girolamo Muziano and Cesare Nebbia are responsible for the decoration of the ceiling, in which they were aided by many other artists. A letter written by Danti to the Flemish cosmographer Abraham Ortelius is very useful in understanding the basic scheme of the frescoes: ". . .having divided Italy in half at the Apennines, I have placed on one side of the gallery that part which is bound by the Ligurian and Tyrrhenian seas, and on the other that which is bound by the Adriatic and the Alps, then subdividing the whole according to the states and the prefectures of the governments into forty parts. . ." The most important cities are portrayed in perspective, as are the battles, in a felicitous figurative blend of history and geography. With reference to the other frescoes, he adds that there are ". . .eighty stories painted on the ceiling of the gallery, above each scene, representing some miracle known to have occurred in the region. . ." So that also on the ceiling we can see the mingling of history, in this case religious, and geography. In 1631, Urban VIII ordered the maps to be completed by the cosmographer Lukas Holste and enriched by new decorations.

46

46. *Library Courtyard. View of the rooms of the Secret Archive and the Tower of Winds.*

47. *Francesco Melloni and Bernardino Cametti: detail of the Monument to Gregory XIII in St. Peter's, showing the reformation of the calendar.*

47

GREGORIO XIII PONT. MAX.

48

The Tower of Winds, the first astronomic observatory of the Vatican, dates from the time of Gregory XIII, and is connected to the reform of the calendar which was introduced by this pope in 1582. It was built above the Gallery of Maps between 1578 and 1580, probably by Ottaviano Mascherino, the architect of the gallery. Overlooking the Library Courtyard, which used to be the middle level of the original Belvedere Courtyard, is a balcony made up of three terraces on different levels. The decoration in the rooms of the tower is the work of Niccolò Circignani, Mattheus Bril, and probably his brother Paul. Niccolò Circignani worked in the loggia which was to be the astronomic observatory, where he painted the personifications of the four winds. On the south wall he painted St. Peter's boat, on the west wall the shipwreck of St. Paul, two themes in a certain way connected with the subject of winds. Mattheus Bril, perhaps with the help of his brother Paul, is the author of the sixty landscapes in the friezes in the other rooms.

The Sistine Library was built by Sixtus V to replace the one built by Sixtus IV, no longer large enough. Having discarded the initial plan to place it in Bramante's Corridor, the pope ordered the construction of a new building where the so-called Belvedere Theatre was. In this way the courtyard was cut in two, losing its unity once and for all. This decision was also taken in order to put a stop to those performances which Sixtus V thought unsuit-

49

48. A room in the Secret Archive, where papal bulls and other documents are kept; since 1881 it is open to scholars.

49. Imperial seals and documents dating from the thirteenth century; these were sent to the popes and are now housed in the Secret Archive.

ed to the dignity of the Apostolic Palace. The project was entrusted to Domenico Fontana in 1587, and in 1588 both the building and its decoration were complete. The speed with which the library was both built and decorated is typical of this pope: a saying of the time was, in fact, that the proverb *Dixit et facta sunt* was to be attributed to Sixtus V. In the eighteenth century the building underwent some changes on the ground floor, as is recorded by the following description by Fontana himself: "... it has enormous loggias on the ground floor, and behind them a very long cellar, above which are fourteen rooms on the second floor (today's Sezione del Catalogo), which will be given to eight men of letters who will always be able to study here...; on the third floor (today's Sala di Consultazione) there are eight rooms for the guardians of the library, and then the library itself (Salone Sistino), which is 318 palms long and 69 wide, with a row of columns in the middle and a vaulted ceiling; it has three rows of windows...; it is all beautifully painted with gold and with many stories..." The iconographical plan of the decoration of this room was arranged by the prefect of the library Federico Ranaldi, while the inscriptions are by the secret servant of the pope,

Guglielmo Bianchi. The chosen themes were two: the glorification of the book through the centuries and the exaltation of the pontificate of Sixtus V. On one side of the library, the libraries of antiquity are portrayed, on the other the ecumenical councils whose task it had been to maintain learning on the road of truth; on the pilasters are the inventors of the letters of the alphabet. On the end wall and in the spaces above the windows are events from the pontificate of Sixtus V. One hundred painters, under the direction of Cesare Nebbia, who drew the cartoons, and Giovanni Guerra, who chose the subject matter, worked on this project. The scenes of Rome are by Paul Bril and Antonio Tempesta.

The so-called Palazzetto del Belvedere was built for Innocent VIII to the north of the Apostolic Palace, on the hill which was known in classical times as *mons sancti Aegidii*. According to Vasari, Antonio del Pollaiuolo designed it, and Cristoforo da Pietrasanta, a Tuscan architect, built it between 1484 and 1487. The construction took place in two distinct phases. At first the building was conceived as a covered place where the pope, walking through the gardens, might stop for a rest. Later it was transformed into a villa. The original building was de-

50. *The Salone Sistino in the Library.*

51. *Palazzetto del Belvedere. North facade. To the left of the crenellated tower is Bramante's Stairway; to the right, the corner of the building housing the Cabinet of Masks.*

52. *Anonymous copy of a drawing by Marten van Heemskerck (1535, detail). The Vatican Hill seen from northwest, looking towards the Palazzetto del Belvedere.*

signed on a rectangular plan; the north facade had a tower on each side of it, a loggia on the ground floor, and a corresponding row of windows above it. The upper part of the building was crowned with "ghibelline" crenellations, rather unusual for a pontifical building, and in great contrast with the residential nature of the construction. The crenellations were on all sides of the palace, even on the south facade, now altered. As in many medieval buildings, the walls overlooking the slope of the hill were supported by massive stonework, with niches, as can be seen in the fresco, probably by Pinturicchio, in the Gallery of Statues. When Innocent VIII decided to transform the building into a villa, a south wing was added to the south-eastern corner. The palace thus became L-shaped, and a few changes were made to the original

53

54

building: two arcades in the eastern side of the loggia today the Gallery of Statues, were walled up to form the rooms of the papal residence; while, to the west, a small chapel with its own sacristy was built. Pinturicchio, who worked here around 1484, and Andrea Mantegna are responsible for the decoration of the Palazzetto del Belvedere. All that is left of the fifteenth century decoration are the frescoes on the ceiling, although later repainted, and the lunettes and fragments of flowers and fruit on the wall opposite the windows in the Gallery of Statues. Between 1488 and 1490 Mantegna frescoed the small chapel which Innocent dedicated to St. John the Baptist. Vasari judged this work as "rather a work of miniature than painting," but there is nothing left of it.

Between the two fifteenth century wings of the palace there was a garden which Julius II decided to convert into his own private museum, open only to artists and men of letters. Donato Bramante worked on this project between 1510 and 1513. He built a wall along the east wing of the palace, joining the north wing to the construction on the right of the Belvedere Courtyard. Parallel to the east wall, he then built a loggia, also connected to both the buildings, creating a square courtyard, which he filled with orange trees. In the four corners he placed the famous statues of the Belvedere Apollo, the Venus Felix, the Tiber and the Laocoon group. Under Pius IV, the loggia of the courtyard was torn down and replaced by Pirro Ligorio with the two-storey building with the Room of the Animals on the ground floor and the Room of the Bronzes of the Gregorian Etruscan Museum on the first floor.

53. *The Courtyard of the Pigna, looking towards the Braccio Nuovo.*

54. *The Courtyard of the Corazze. The base of the Colonna Antonina and the Atrium of the Four Gates.*

55. *The Courtyard of the Pigna, looking towards Pirro Ligorio's Nicchione.*

56. *The Octagonal Courtyard.*

57

The Pio-Clementine Museum was begun by Clement XIV and completed by Pius VI. This museum incorporated, with slight alterations, the rooms of the Palazzetto of Innocent VIII and of the building of Pirro Ligorio, and led to the construction of new extensions. The first project was given, in 1771, to the architect Alessandro Dori who only made a very few changes; he transformed the loggia of the Palazzetto del Belvedere into the Gallery of Statues, and demolished the dividing walls of the east wing, replacing them with the present arches which form the Room of the Busts, where Innocent VIII's small chambers had been. He also enlarged the west wing where the Cabinet of Masks now is. In 1772, Michelangelo Simonetti was given the task of redesigning the contiguous Courtyard of the Oranges, giving it a portico. The architect followed the square plan of Bramante's courtyard, with its flattened corners, and made the octagonal portico, from which the present courtyard derives its name. The entrance was at the end of the Chiaramonti Gallery. On 12 May 1776, Pius VI decided that "this impressive construction should be completed by the addition of two more wings which would end in a round atrium, with

57. Bramante's Stairway in the Palazzetto del Belvedere.

58. The Gallery of Statues in the Palazzetto del Belvedere.

59. Egyptian Museum. Statue of Amun-Ra.

60. Pio-Clementine Museum. Belvedere Apollo.

61. Gregorian Etruscan Museum. The Mars of Todi.

access to the library." This task was intrusted to Simonetti, who was succeeded at his death (1787) by his pupil Giuseppe Camporese, whose masterpiece is the Atrium of the Four Gates. The works began with the demolition of the Mantegna chapel in order to prolong the Gallery of Statues. The room, at that time known as the Room of the Torso, was enlarged to the north and became the Room of the Animals. This room derives its name from the statues of animals, all classical but restored by Francesco Antonio Franzoni. This room was part of the build-

58

59

60

61

62

63

62. *Pinacoteca. View of the Octagonal Room.*

63. *Pinacoteca. The facade overlooking the Square Garden.*

64. *Gregorian Profane Museum. View of a room.*

65. *The exterior of the new museums, the Gregorian Profane and the Pio-Christian. In the background, the Atrium of the Four Gates.*

ing of Pirro Ligorio, and now houses the statue of Meleager. Lastly, the west wing of the Gallery of Statues was transformed into the Cabinet of Masks, a typical eighteenth century museum.

The Gregorian Etruscan Museum, 1837, and the Gregorian Egyptian Museum, 1839, both founded by Gregory XVI, are housed in the buildings behind the Nicchione by Pirro Ligorio, and in the side wings, built under Julius II, Julius III and Pius IV by Bramante, Girolamo da Carpi and Pirro Ligorio, which partially overlook the Octagonal Courtyard.

The Etruscan Museum, which also spreads to the upper floor of the Palazzetto del Belvedere, has a collection of objects for the most part found in the necropoles of southern Etruria, in private digs licensed by the Pontifical Government.

The Egyptian Museum is important not only for the objects it exhibits, but also for the attempt, at the time unheard of, to recreate entire rooms. The new arrangement of the museum, which strictly follows modern theories, has very rightly respected the romantic, naive, but for the time very daring, nineteenth century pseudo-Egyptian decoration by Giuseppe de Fabris.

One of the most recent constructions in the Vatican, inaugurated in 1970, now houses the collections formerly in the Lateran. These include the Gregorian Profane Museum, the Pio-Christian Museum and the Missionary-Ethnological Museum. The

64

Gregory Profane Museum was set up by Gregory XVI in 1844 and includes mainly ancient sculptures, copies and remodellings of classical Greek originals and also Roman sculptures from the late republican and imperial eras. The Pio-Christian Museum was founded by Pius IX in 1854. In it are collected works of early Christian art, particularly sarcophagi and inscriptions. Lastly, the Missionary-Ethnological Museum was set up by Pius XI in 1927 and houses documents of religions other than the Christian, of non-European art and cultures. According to the wishes of John XXIII, these museums were transferred to a building to the north of the Pinacoteca. Begun in 1963-1964 by Vatican architects, this building was then transformed between 1964 and 1971 by the architectural firm of the Passarelli brothers. The south wall, with its squat and protruding arches, is reminiscent of the earlier "wall of the spinster." The interior consists of one large room. The Gregorian Profane Museum is on the ground floor, while the Pio-Christian is raised on a sort of balcony on the same floor. Metal trellisses are the dividing walls, and metal tubes form the pedestals of the sculptures, enhancing even more their shape and form in the contrast with these amorphous objects. The arrangement of the material is didactic as it is in the Missionary-Ethnological Museum, on the floor beneath.

The Historical Museum, opened to the public in 1973, was set up below the so-called Square Garden

65

next to the Pinacoteca. The carriages and other means of transport used by the popes and by their following, from the nineteenth century till the present day, are exhibited in this museum, together with various uniforms and relics of the papal armed forces, disbanded in 1970.

The Hall of Papal Audiences is another very recent construction, designed by Pier Luigi Nervi in 1964 and inaugurated in 1971. It can hold 12,000 people and is shell-shaped. The immense vaulted ceiling is structurally bound to the concave gallery, forming a solid body which almost "floats" on the unsteady ground.

66. *Pio-Christian Museum. The Good Shepherd.*

67. *Historical Museum. The Mercedes Benz used by Pius XII.*

68. *Missionary-Ethnological Museum. Statue of Bhima, the benevolent demon (southern India).*

69. *Pier Luigi Nervi: the Hall of Papal Audiences.*

70. *The apse and dome of St. Peter's, seen from the Vatican Gardens.*

The Vatican Gardens

The Vatican Gardens were first mentioned during the papacy of Innocent IV (1243-1254). At that time it was more of a vineyard or an orchard rather than a garden, near the Papal Palace.

By the time of Nicholas III (1277-1280) a real garden (*viridarium, jardinum*) was referred to as "thickly planted with many different kinds of trees," near the orchard (*pomerium*); there was a small lawn (*pratellum*) and a fountain in the garden extending to *mons Sancti Aegidii,* which was enclosed by a wall during the second year of that pontificate (1279). At the crest of the hill was the *Viridaria* gate. Simone da Genova, the doctor of Nicholas IV (1288-1292), was the first to grow medicinal herbs in this garden. This was several centuries before the institution of botanical studies at Padova, Bologna, or Pisa universities.

The popes devoted attention to this first Vatican garden even after the apostolic see was transferred to Avignon. In fact, in 1365, Urban V gave orders to his vicar at Rome, the bishop of Orvieto, to "cultivate the garden and fill it with good vines and a variety of flowering and fruit trees." This work was carried out. Particular care was given to developing a vineyard which (it was hoped) would produce 300 casks of wine a year. In 1370 the pope authorized the payment of 6,621 Florins for expenses encountered in producing the vineyard and fishpond in "our garden near St. Peter's palace."

A custodian was appointed to this garden and vineyard, and in 1371 the task was entrusted to Giovanni Chambaret, a Grey Friar.

Further mention of the garden-orchard is not made

71

72

73

71. *Aerial view of the Vatican Gardens. In the foreground, the Rampart of the Heliport; at the center, the crenellated Leonine walls with the Tower of St. John on the right and the Radio Tower on the left; behind the Leonine walls, the Vatican Broadcasting Center (Palazzina Marconi), the Ethiopian College, the Palace of the Government, the Railway Station (right); to the right of the transept, Piazza Santa Marta, the Sacristy and the cement roof of the Hall of Papal Audiences.*

72. *Arco delle Campane, through which one reaches the Vatican Gardens.*

73. *The Teutonic College.*

74. *Ignazio Danti: map of Rome (1580) in the Gallery of Maps. Detail of the Vatican.*

until the middle of the next century. Nicholas V (1447-1455) had planned to plant new vineyards, but this was not done until the time of Pius II (1458-1464) who refashioned the arbors and the viridarium.

The renovation continued under Innocent VIII (1484-1492) who had a small palace, the Palazzetto, built on *mons Sancti Aegidii* for the popes' relaxation. Antonio Pollaiuolo designed the palace which was built by Jacopo da Pietrasanta.

Orange trees were planted in the courtyard where Julius II (1503-1513) placed his famous sculpture collection. Outside the palace was a garden with cypresses and ancient sculptures. Not far away was the *Galinarium* with a tower still standing today.

Under Julius II, Bramante connected Innocent VIII's Palazzetto del Belvedere to the Apostolic Palace by means of a raised road, and arranged the area between the two buildings on three levels, two of them with a garden joined by staircases.

43

75. *The fountain in Piazza Santa Marta.*

76. *Piazza Santa Marta with the transept of St. Peter's and the Sacristy.*

Clement VII (1523-1534) embellished with flower beds the so-called Zitella area, located between the Vatican walls and what was later to become the Square Garden adjacent to the Palazzetto del Belvedere.

Under Paul III (1534-1549) it was decided to make full use of the garden area and "to level the land where His Holiness wants to make a new garden"; this was to become the Square Garden (formerly called the "Secret" Garden) and had covered paths laid out in the shape of a cross. Supervisor of the works was the architect Jacopo Meleghino, and in fact, in a map of Rome by Leonardo Bufalini (1551), the garden is sketched out and the "woods" are also indicated.

Under Julius III (1550-1555) a fishpond was added, which was replaced by the Fountain of the Galley in the following century.

In 1558 Pirro Ligorio began Casina Pia for Paul IV (1555-1559), completed later under his successor Pius IV (1559-1565). Pius V (1566-1572) was responsible for the development of a Herb Garden in that area; Monsignor Michele Mercati was the first "herbalist of Our Lord."

Under Gregory XIII (1572-1585) the Garden was extended to the crest of Vatican Hill and included a woody area planted with olive trees, ilex, oaks, and laurel.

The Gardens, as they were in 1574, can be seen in a painting by Mario Cartaro. Beginning in the east, they are as follows: the Garden with the fishpond of Julius III (later, the Galley Fountain) below Bramante's Corridor; the inner gardens (later called the Pigna Gardens) and those of the Library and Statues; the Vatican Garden properly speaking, including the Secret Garden (later called Square Garden) laid out under Paul III; the Gardens around the Casina of Pius IV, among which is the Garden of Herbs commissioned by Pius V in the area adjacent to the Stradone di Belvedere; the woods extending to St. John's

Tower, dating from the time of Gregory XIII. To the north, near the walls, was the *galinarium* or "hen house," with a garden next to it, set up during Clement VII's time.

Under Sixtus V (1585-1590) the Acqua Felice aqueduct was diverted into the Vatican, enabling the fishponds and fountains to be constructed.

The work was completed by Paul V (1605-1621), during whose pontificate the Acqua Paola aqueduct was brought to Rome; the fountains of the Towers (or the Sacrament), the Aquilone (or Scoglio), and the Galley were then built. The fountain in the center of the Belvedere Courtyard was also built at this time by Carlo Maderno. Also under Paul V the Library Courtyard was planted with citrus trees; other plantations of citrus fruit were made in the gardens reached by the Stradone di Belvedere.

In 1676 the Secret Garden of Paul III was enlarged and renamed the Square Garden; later on Clement XI (1700-1721) had the Courtyard of the Pigna remade into an Italian garden. The potted citrus trees still stand on bases bearing the Papal coat of arms.

Pius VI (1775-1799) created an access to the Gardens from the Atrium of the Four Gates. He also constructed a gate by the woods near the shrine of the Madonna della Guardia where, up to the time of Leo XIII, the Gardens properly began. In addition, he created a new back-drop for the Fountain of the Galley (1779).

Gregory XVI (1831-1846) made an important addition to the Gardens. This pope raised the surrounding wall and created a monumental new access to the Stradone di Belvedere; he modified the Square Garden by placing a fountain in the center, by adding 224 pots of citrus trees, and by having his coat of arms designed in the flower beds. He also transformed a woody area into an English garden according to nineteenth century taste, with ponds and false ruins, and changed the surroundings of Pius IV's Casina. Inside the walls

77. *The church of Santo Stefano degli Abissini.*

78. *The portal of Santo Stefano degli Abissini.*

near the entrance to the Belvedere Courtyard the meadows were leveled, planted with trees, and made into a public park.

Works of various kinds were completed by subsequent popes. Leo XIII (1878-1903) added a modest palazzina for the Papal summer residence and a replica of the Lourdes Grotto during his pontificate. Then Saint Pius X (1903-1914) had a tunnel dug to form a passage from the Belvedere Courtyard to the Gardens. He also had a Gothic style chapel built above the Lourdes Grotto (later demolished). Benedict XV (1914-1922) contributed the little shrine of the Madonna della Guardia and had two greenhouses built in the Square Garden. Finally, Pius XI (1922-1939) reorganized the gardens after the creation of the Vatican State in 1929. Some of the most important buildings of the State were erected in their surroundings, such as the Palace of the Government (1930), the Railway Station, the Radio-telegraph station, the School of Mosaic, the Ethiopian College, and the Pinacoteca located in part of the Square Garden. During this pontificate the remains of the monument commemorating the First Vatican Ecumenical Council and a Chinese pergola presented by Chinese Catholics in 1933 were displayed in the gardens.

Under John XXIII (1958-1963) St. John's Tower was adapted as a papal summer residence. Next to it, under Paul VI (1963-1978), the Heliport was built, from which the present pope sets out on his pastoral travels and on his journeys to Castel Gandolfo.

During the time of John XXIII and Paul VI a new museum was built on Zitella avenue to house the collections formerly in the Lateran. These include the Gregorian Profane Museum, the Pio-Christian Museum, and the Missionary-Ethnological Museum. In the same period a new Historical Museum was established in an area created specifically for it underneath the Square Garden.

The usual entrance to the Vatican Gardens is from Piazza Santa Marta. This square is between the Sacristy and St. Peter's Rectory, the Palazzo di San Carlo, the Palazzo del Tribunale (the old Vatican Seminary), and St. Peter's Basilica. In the center of Piazza Santa Marta is a garden with a fountain and some beautiful magnolia, ilex, and cypress trees trained and pruned in traditional elegant geometrical forms.

The Church of Santo Stefano Maggiore, also called Santo Stefano degli Abissini, built before the eighth century, was restored by Leo III (795-816). In 1439 Eugene IV gave it to the "Indians" and from then on it was called Santo Stefano degli Abissini. Coptic monks had a charitable institution next to it beginning in 1479. From 1919 to 1931 it was the Ethiopian Pontifical College (see below). This church, restored by Clement XI in 1706, has an important twelfth-century Romanesque portal and preserves the basilica plan of three aisles divided by columns.

In the flower beds next to this church are two young, flourishing *Ginkgo biloba* plants; this conifer of Chinese origin existed in Mesozoic times. It is considered sacred in China and perhaps owes its survival to this tradition. Near the church are some very hardy examples of Araucarias (or monkey-puzzles) that stand out because of their dissimilarity to other plants in the Gardens. These are *Araucaria bidwillii* whose natural habitat is Australia, known there by the name of bunya. They grow well in a mild rainy climate.

The School of Mosaic was established at the end of the sixteenth century for the decoration of the new Vatican Basilica. It was officially organized in the third decade of the eighteenth century by Pietro Paolo Cristofari, who in 1727 was appointed superintendent in charge of the "mosaic painters" who worked on St. Peter's. At that time the first group of mosaicists were employed and they worked regularly in the factory, producing mosaic copies of all altar paintings and other decorative works in St. Peter's. The production of the School also included the miniature mosaic

79. The Railway Station.

80. The Mosaic School.

81. The Palace of the Government.

82. The Fountain of the Shell.

83-84. The Fontana della Scogliera with Arum Lilies (below) and Agave.

85. An Ash-leaved Maple on Viale dell'Osservatorio.

86. Crassula arborescens among the rocks of the Scogliera.

pictures offered as gifts to visiting dignitaries to Rome.

The Vatican School of Mosaic continues to function in this new location, to which it was transferred in 1931.

The Vatican Railway Station, built on a design by the architect Giuseppe Momo (Vercelli 1876-1940) and inaugurated in 1930, is linked to the Rome–Viterbo line by a viaduct and is used for receiving and sending goods from the Vatican.

On 4 October 1962 John XXIII began his pilgrimage to Assisi and Loreto from here; the present pope, John Paul II, departed from the Vatican Railway Station for a trip around Rome on 8 November 1979.

Two bas-reliefs by Edoardo Rubino (Turin 1871-1954) decorate the outer wall. One shows the Miraculous Draught of Fishes and the other the Prophet Elijah on the Chariot of Fire.

On the green slope of Vatican Hill is the Fountain of the Shell, surrounded by a low border of Box hedge (*Buxus sempervirens*); in the background there is a remarkable variety of evergreens: *Pinus, Cupressus, Cedrus, Chamaecyparis, Juniperus, Picea.* There are

evergreens everywhere. Often of diverse and even rare species, an intense green color is maintained even during the winter months. Among the flowering trees, the most spectacular are the Magnolias, especially the ones with the large white flowers. Some have even been pruned into a conical shape.

The Palace of the Government, built in 1928-1931 from plans by Giuseppe Momo, houses the main offices for the administration of the Vatican City: the Papal Commission for the State with its President, Vice-president, and Special Delegate; the Council of the State; the Governor, the General Management of Technical and Economic Services.

The chapel of Santa Marta (named after a church demolished in 1930) is connected to the Palace. It stands behind the apse of St. Peter's near Santo Stefano degli Abissini.

On its altar is a painted crucifix, the work of Alessandro Algardi (around 1644) and donated by him to the Rector and Chaplain of Santa Marta, Father Vincenzo Monticelli in 1653.

Next to the Palace of the Government are some beautiful examples of *Nolina longifolia*, a woody plant of Mexican origin, of the Agave family.

82

84

83

86

85

87

88

From the large square in front of the Palace one has an excellent view of St. Peter's dome.

On the grassy slopes below, the papal coat of arms is formed by different botanical species in various shades of green.

At different times of the year flowering plants make the design more complete. The *Buxus* and the *Evonymus*, in different shades of green compose the background of the shield, while the annuals (for example, the *Ageratum houstonianum* from Mexico) serve to complete the heraldic symbols of the tiara and the keys.

Viale dell'Osservatorio flanks an artificial cliff, interrupted by a fountain, with small, varied decorative plants worthy of special attention. A great variety and abundance of plant life can be observed here; at certain times of the year the rocky slopes are covered in flowers, creating a particularly pleasant effect.

Starting at the left there are Centaurea with their blue-green leaves, Broom (*Cytisus scoparius*), Cordyline with lance-like leaves forming a thick tuft, a bush of Rosemary (*Rosmarinus officinalis*), a characteristic Mediterranean bush, *Setcreasea purpurea* with dark red leaves and delicate pink flowers, a creeping variety from Mexico. There are also an orange and yellow kind of Gazania; Aloe with tall, single, orange-colored blossoms of various shades, nearly all from Africa; *Senecia repens* with silvery leaves, suitable for the dry South African climate; a group of pretty white Daisies (*Chrysanthemum frutescens*); the subtropical *Crassula arborescens*; Fuchsia, a hybrid originally form Peru; *Saxifraga, Bergenia stachey*, whose natural habitat is 4000 meters above sea level in the north-east Himalayas; Agave, originally from Mexico.

Around the fountain grow white funnel-shaped Arum Lilies (*Zantedeschia aethiopica*), Alocasias, Begonias, from the humid tropics, Maidenhair fern (*Adiantum capillus Veneris*), the graceful and elegant herbaceous rockplants with delicate little green leaves.

On the cliff are *Dasylirion* with their characteristic serrated edge leaves, Asparagus (*Asparagus scendens deflexus*) of South Africa origin, different species of *Cotoneaster* from China that have enriched our gardens with spiny, very solidly colored, bushes with

87. The monument to the First Vatican Ecumenical Council and the Gardener's House, seen from the dome of St. Peter's.

88. The Ethiopian College.

numerous small berries. Almost by chance one occasionally sees splendid little Rose bowers with a variety of prize roses which are quite a remarkable sight of color and beauty when in bloom.

At the end of Viale dell'Osservatorio are the remains of the commemorative monument of the First Vatican Ecumenical Council. In 1869 Pius IX commissioned this monument from Virginio Vespignani; it was to stand in front of San Pietro in Montorio. The end of the popes' temporal power and the new political situation in Rome and all Italy prevented the inauguration of the monument, although it was finished.

In 1885, under the reign of Leo XIII, it was set up in the middle of the Courtyard of the Pigna; it consisted of a square base with bas-reliefs mounted on a second circular base supporting an ancient column of African marble. On this column was a bronze statue of St. Peter. This monument, already reduced in height by the removal of the damaged column, was transferred to the Gardens in 1936 where it underwent further modification.

The bronze statue is by Filippo Gnaccarini; on the base of the statue are inscriptions by Pius IX (1871) and Leo XIII (1885), bas-reliefs representing "A Council Meeting" (Pietro Galli), the coat of arms of Pius IX and Leo XIII, and the allegorical figures of Wisdom and the Syllabus. Additional fragments are placed around the monument, where there are also some specimens of *Phoenix canariensis* framing an exceptional view of St. Peter's dome.

Still following Viale dell'Osservatorio, one sees in the flower bed on the right an example of Melaleuca, the slow-growing evergreen myrtle, as well as several examples of *Cupressus arizonica*. In the background, near the Vatican Radio Station, is a Bougainvillea originally from Brasil, with its leafy bract of brightly colored violet almost entirely covering the wall. On

89. *The Fontana della Barchetta with an Oleander.*

90. *The Lourdes Grotto.*

the slope below are Mediterranean Cypresses, Maples (*Acer negundo variegatum*), more Magnolias, Palms, and so forth.

The Ethiopian College and the Camposanto Teutonico are the only two medieval and Renaissance institutions left in Vatican City.

The College was once annexed to the church of Santo Stefano degli Abissini located behind the apse of the Vatican Basilica.

This church, restored in the eighth century by Leo III, was donated to the Coptic monks by Sixtus IV in 1479. In 1919 Benedict XV transformed it into the Papal Ethiopian College; Pius XI provided the College with a new and more suitable location, begun in 1928 after a plan by Giuseppe Momo and completed in 1931.

Near the College the Fontana della Barchetta is surrounded with Oleanders (*Nerium oleander*) of Mediterranean origin and a group of Banana trees (*Musa*). Near these grow bushes of Lilac (*Syringa vulgaris*) and sour oranges of the bitter variety (*Citrus aurantium var. amara*).

A replica of the Lourdes Grotto stands in a large square of the same name. It was given to Leo XIII in 1902 by the Bishop of Tarbes, of Lourdes diocese. This is a reproduction of the famous Grotto at Massabielle where the Madonna appeared to St. Bernadette Soubirous in 1858.

It is decorated with mosaic portraits of Leo XIII, Pius X, and Monsignor Francis Xavier Schoepfer, Bishop of Tarbes.

Pius X had a Gothic style cusp erected above the Grotto that was destroyed in 1933.

The original altar from the Grotto of Massabielle, presented to John XXIII, is in the Vatican and is used on special occasions.

Inscriptions composed by Monsignor Schoepfer refer to the gift of the replica to Leo XIII and to the difficult situation in France at that time.

Also inscribed are the Virgin's words to Bernadette: "Allez boire à la fontaine et vous y laver," with the date, 25 february 1858. Several kinds of climbing liana cover the front of the Grotto: Ivy (*Hedera helix*), *Ampelopsis, Parthenocissus tricuspidata.*

In front of it is a flower bed with *Cycas revoluta*, a plant resembling the palm, but of a very ancient kind belonging to the *Cycadalae* family and considered a living fossil.

The avenue named after Pius XI passes among beds full of rare and precious conifers: the genus *Picea*, the genus *Chamaecyparis*, the *Cupressus* of the *Lawsoniana* species, *Juniperus* in tree and shrub form. Contrasting with the many greens is a delicate Maple (*Acer palmatum athropurpureum*) of Japanese origin, with its beautiful red color, and its graceful, elegant shape.

The stretch of wall surrounding the Vatican Gardens belongs to the first enclosure of the Vatican and was erected under Leo IV (847-855) for the defense of St. Peter's against Saracen raids. It was renovated at the time of Nicholas V (1447-1455) and further restored in recent times.

The wall began at Castel Sant'Angelo, near where *Porta Sancti Angeli* once was, following the route of the Corridoio di Borgo as far as the Vatican Palace where there was a second gate called San Pellegrino or *Sancti Petri*, located behind the arc of columns to the right of St. Peter's Square. Near this was the tower of

91

92

93

91. *A Japanese Maple.*

92. *The Italian Garden and the Vatican Broadcasting Center (Palazzina Marconi).*

93. *The Italian Garden with its typical Box hedges.*

94. *The Vatican Gardens, seen from Largo della Capanna Cinese, towards St. Peter's.*

Nicholas V, an imposing means of protection, now much reduced in height.

From here the wall, rebuilt by Nicholas V, continued to the Vatican Palaces, crossing the Belvedere Courtyard and leading up to the gardens where above, at the Zecca (the Mint), the remains of the earliest parts are preserved.

The last stretch, remarkably well preserved, dates from the time of Nicholas V and includes two round towers, known as Radio Tower and St. John's Tower; then, following approximately the course of the outer wall, climbed up Monte Santo Spirito and reached the Tiber. Near the present Santo Spirito gate was the *Posterula Saxonum.*

Below Via Pio XI is the Marconi Radio Station, established by Pius XI to ensure the independence of the Holy See and at the same time to assist apostolic work.

The first plans were designed by Guglielmo Marconi and carried out by the Marconi Society of London; it was provided with Greek Franklin antennas and was considered to be ahead of its time. Inauguration of the Marconi Radio Station took place on 12 February 1931 in the presence of Pius XI, Guglielmo Marconi, and numerous Vatican officials. Its first director was Father Giuseppe Gianfranceschi, a well-

94

known scientist who in 1929 had participated in the polar expedition of Umberto Nobile.

In front of the building, looking from the terrace, one sees the Italian garden with flower beds bordered by *Buxus sempervirens*. Outstanding in this Italian garden are some huge and ancient Palm trees. There are also many clumps of miniature Palms, also called St. Peter's palms (*Chamaerops humilis*), which grow in the Mediterranean area; bluish Butia palms, tall, slender Washingtonia originally from California and Arizona; examples of Livistona and other varieties already mentioned.

To the right, outstanding in its proud and majestic appearance, is a beautiful Beech (*Fagus sylvatica*) that normally grows at an altitude of more than 1000 meters above sea level.

Walking to the right one passes the Shrine of St. Theresa, built at the time of Pius XII (1939-1958), and close to a wall completely covered with *Ficus pumilia*. Note also the characteristic *Cotoneaster salicifolium* and the creeping *Juniperus chinensis* in the flower bed. One then reaches Largo della Capanna Cinese which presents a beautiful view of the dome of St. Peter's.

St. John's Rampart is part of the fortified wall of the Vatican, the sector of the Roman wall that girds the Vatican Gardens along two sides. This part of the wall was begun after the Sack of 1527, taking advantage of new advances in military architecture.

The work was entrusted to Antonio da Sangallo the Younger who first built the Santo Spirito Rampart and its gate, left unfinished in 1544; it was followed by the construction of the Belvedere Rampart designed by Michelangelo (1547).

The wall was completed at the time of Pius IV (1559-1565) under the direction of the military architect Francesco Laparelli and new gates were opened in the enclosure, such as the Pertusa (today walled up) in the center of the stretch of wall between the St. John Rampart and the Heliport.

In the large square is a marble statue of St. Bernard (1090-1153) by an unknown artist. The saint holds his most famous work in his hand, *De Consideratione*, dedicated to Eugene III.

Along Viale Pio XII, in the garden with the Vatican Radio antenna, one can enjoy in the springtime two columns completely covered in Wisteria (*Wisteria sinensis*). Here there is also the bronze statue of Blessed Urban (1088-1099), promoter of the Crusades, donated by the French diocese of Reims to Leo XIII (1887). It is a copy of the monument erected to this pope in Chatillon-sur-Marne.

St. John's Tower is part of the wall surrounding the Leonine city, but was rebuilt at the time of Nicholas V (1447-1455). In recent times it was restored and remodelled as a summer home for John XXIII (1958-1963).

95

96

97

98

95. *The Shrine of St. Theresa and a Butia Palm.*

96. *The Tower of St. John and various examples of Palms.*

97. *The Tower of St. John and the Leonine walls.*

98. *The statue of Urban II.*

In 1967 the Patriarch of Constantinople, Athenagoras, was a guest there during his visit to the Vatican.

The Heliport, located on the rampart of the same name, was constructed in 1976 by Paul VI. It is used by the pope for travelling by helicopter to Castel Gandolfo and to other places near the Vatican when practical.

In the flower bed opposite, at the entrance to Viale degli Olivi, there are rare examples of Mugho Pine (*Pinus mugo*, low spreading variety) which grows naturally in the highest mountains of Europe.

In the gardens next to Viale degli Olivi there is a monument commemorating the appearance of the Madonna of Guadalupe to an Indian in 1531, by A. Ponzanelli. It was given to Pius XII by the Mexican government and was inaugurated on 21 September 1939.

Next to this monument is the Fountain of the Frogs with beautiful white Waterlilies (*Nymphaea alba*) floating on the water. The fountain makes use of an

99

100

99. The monument to the Madonna of Guadalupe.

100. The Fountain of the Frogs.

101. The statue of St. Austremonius.

102. The statue of the Madonna of Fatima.

101

102

ancient amphora for its water supply.

Around the fountain tall trees, shrubs and decorative flowers placed in pots are arranged to complement the design of the paths around the monument.

Here one sees Magnolias, Cycads, Cedars, shrubs with thick sweet-smelling flowers like Buddleia, Lagestroemia, Holly (*Ilex aquifolium*), Cherry Laurel (*Prunus laurocerasus*) and *Cocculus laurifolius*, a Himalayan evergreen. A Camphor tree (*Cinnamomum Camphora*), an evergreen of Japanese and Chinese origin, towers over the latter.

The potted plants include Gardenias, Hydrangeas, Azaleas; in the beds are Begonias, Tagetes, Violets, Petunias, Asters, Ageratum or Flossflower, Cyclamens, alternately blooming according to the season.

At the end of the Viale degli Olivi is a statue of the Madonna of Fatima by Frederick Shradi (New York, 1907). It was donated by the sculptor and inaugurated by John Paul II on 13 May 1983.

In the center of the Lourdes Grotto square is the bronze statue of St. Austremonius, Bishop of Cler-mont and first bishop of the church of Auvergne (fourth century), given to Leo XIII by a group of pilgrims from that region in 1887.

Flower beds border the Leonine wall. On either side of a central path, one finds Hydrangeas on the right, and borders of Kaffir Lilies and Aralias (*Fatsia japonica*, of Japanese origin).

The building which houses the Vatican Radio Station includes one of the towers of the Leonine walls in its fifteenth-century reconstruction (Radio Tower). The Vatican Observatory was located here from 1919 to 1933. The Observatory was previously in the Tower of the Winds and was later transferred to the Papal Palace of Castel Gandolfo.

The ceiling of the main room of the tower was frescoed by Ludwig Seitz (1844-1908) who, in honor of Leo XIII, reproduced the constellation of Leo.

Next to this is the Palazzina of Leo XIII (1878-1903), a modest summer home used as a resting place by this pontiff, near the tower now called Radio Tower. It was connected by an iron footbridge to the Leonine walls. The first offices of the Vatican Radio were opened here in 1939.

Through a gate built by Pius VI in 1787 one enters the Woods. Since the mid-sixteenth century one part of the Gardens had been left in its natural state: a woodlands. Later on, paths were made and it was subsequently embellished with statues and fountains.

One may observe here plants introduced through the centuries, for example the *Prunus triloba*, of Chinese origin, the *Pittosporum tobira*, the Aralia and the *Berberis thumbergi* of a golden purple variety. The Woods preserve a typical Mediterranean character, consisting mainly of Oaks of different species: the Holm-oak (*Quercus ilex*) and other oaks such as Common Oak, Pubescent Oak, and so on. In addition there are Poplars, Plane trees, Maples, Judas trees and Acacias.

Typical Mediterranean bushes of Box, Viburnum, and Privet constitute the underbrush. There is also an abundance of wild flowers, such as Iris, Freesia, Acanthus, Crocus, Primrose, Narcissus.

The little shrine of the Madonna della Guardia, a replica of a statue in the entrance to the port of Genoa, recalls the apparition of the Virgin to the pea-

103. The palazzina of Leo XIII with the Radio Tower.

104. The Chalet of Leo XIII with the Radio Tower.

105-109. The Woods: the little shrine of the Madonna della Guardia (106), the statue of St. Peter in Chains (107), the statue of St. Albin stopping Attila (108), and the Chinese Hut (109).

sant Pareto. It was donated to Benedict XV (1914-1922) by the city of Genoa.

Inside the Woods one can see the following monuments: St. Peter in Chains, a marble statue by Amalia Dupré (Florence, 1843-1929), donated to Leo XIII by the Calasanzian order in 1887; St. Albin, Bishop of Châlons-sur-Marne (fifth century) stopping Attila, invader of Gaul, a bronze group given to Leo XIII by the diocese of Châlons-sur-Marne; the Capanna Cinese, or Chinese hut, donated to Pius XI in 1933. Throughout the woods and at its edges are numerous little fountains, some commissioned by Benedict XV (1914-1922), who personally supervised the many details in the arrangement of the gardens, both in regard to the fountains and the paths in the woods.

One of the most charming fountains is the Fontana delle Cascatelle. Also in the woods are various sculptures, inscriptions, and ancient columns.

The Fountain of the Scoglio, or Aquilone, was built in 1611-12 by Martino Ferrabosco and Jan van Xanten.

The eagle, accompanied by dragons, dominates the picturesque composition made up of a series of artificial grottos. The eagle is a reference to the coat of arms of the reigning pope, Paul V Borghese (1605-1621).

The triton to the right, reminiscent of Bernini's fountain of the same name, is the work of Stefano Maderno.

The fountain was intended as a showpiece for the Acqua Paola aqueduct that Paul V had had built from Lake Bracciano to the Vatican, restoring the aqueduct of Trajan (*Aqua Traiana*).

From the avenue of the Square Garden, some steps lead down the hillside; here there are bushes of Myrtle (*Myrtus communis*), an example of *Thuiasis dolobrata*, of Japanese origin, a row of Agave, and splendid examples of Palms of the *Butia, Phoenix* and *Livistona* genus.

A small square leads to the rear entrance of a modern building which houses the Papal Academy of Science adjoining the Casina of Pius IV (special permission required to visit), from which one can see the elliptical Courtyard that the Casina and the Loggia look out upon.

The Casina of Pius IV was conceived as a retreat for the pontiffs, much like the Belvedere which was used by Innocent VIII and the one used by Julius III near Bramante's Nicchione. Its construction was begun by Pirro Ligorio for Paul IV in 1558; after his death it was completed by his successor Pius IV, who placed a commemorative inscription on it in 1561. Decoration of the interior continued after this date.

The Casina is one of the most characteristic examples of Mannerist architecture in Italy, consisting of three fundamental parts: the Casina itself, the Courtyard, and the Loggia. The entrance is from the elliptical Courtyard that unites the other two architectural

110

111

112

113

110. *The Fontana dell'Aquilone.*

111, 112. *The Fountain of the Triton and the Fountain of the Siren, in the rose bower.*

113. *Detail of the Fountain of the Sacrament, showing the dragon of the Borghese family coat-of-arms.*

114. *The Fountain of the Sacrament.*

elements; the entrance is reached by passing through a double aedicula decorated with mosaics that curve toward the interior to follow the shape of the Courtyard, introducing styles belonging to the Baroque. The decoration consists of pots placed on the surrounding walls, while in the center is a fountain by Niccolò Bresciani (1560) decked with small marble statues by Jacopo da Casignola. Rich scenes in stucco decorate the Casina and Loggia facing the Courtyard.

The facade of the villa has a portico with columns repeating the lines of the Loggia. Above this is a row of stuccoes by Rocco da Montefiascone, the principal scenes showing Pan, Cyparissus, Aegle, Sol and the Three Hours; in the center is the commemorative inscription and the coat of arms of Pius IV. Also represented are the coat of arms of officials of his court: Federico Borromeo, General of the Church; Cardinal P. Francesco Ferreri; Cardinal G. Antonio Serbelloni; Cardinal Giovanni de' Medici; Gabrio Serbelloni, Commander of the Papal Guard; and G. B. Serbelloni, Governor of Castel Sant'Angelo.

The facade of the Loggia is completely decorated

PAV·LVS·V·PONTIFEX·MAXIMVS
AD·AVGENDVM·PALATII·PROSPECTVS
ET·HORTORVM·DECOREM
FIERI·IVSSIT·PONT·ANNO·IV

115

with scenes in stucco, showing Apollo with the Muses and Dawn's Chariot. A rich pavement of colored marble covers the interior that looks out on an open gallery with columns toward the Courtyard and in another direction toward the gardens. The barrel vault is decorated with sculpture by Rocco da Montefiascone (1561) and with small frescoes of the life of Moses and mythological scenes by Federico Zuccari and Lorenzo Costa (1563). At either end are two small fountains. Beyond the Loggia toward the garden is a fishpond, about which more will be said later.

The vestibule of the Casina has a shape similar to the Loggia and its walls are decorated in a variety of materials.

The vault has stuccoes that frame frescoes of stories from Genesis; in an oval is God the Father.

The rooms on the ground floor have ceilings with stucco work framing paintings by Federico Zuccari, Santi di Tito, Federico Barocci and others. In the center of the ceiling is the Holy Family by Barocci and Pierleone Genga; around this are allegorical figures. In the second room there is a beautiful Annunciation by Federico Barocci. On the stairway Santi di Tito has painted scenes of papal residences. The rooms on the first floor were decorated by Santi di Tito, Federico Zuccari, Orazio Sammachini and Lor-

enzo Costa. Tommaso Boscoli did the stuccoes; in the Gallery there is the coat of arms of Gregory XIV (1590-91).

The building was originally very small but was enlarged, particularly at the back, after the Papal Academy of Science moved there in 1922.

The Academy is part of the Lincei Academy founded in 1603 by Federico Cesi and others, restored by Pius IX under the name of the Papal Academy of the New Lincei, enlarged by Leo XIII in 1887, and refounded with a new statute by Pius XI in 1930.

Its members are seventy academics in the fields of physical and natural sciences, famous throughout the world.

Below the Casina of Pius IV is the Piazzale degli Obelischi, arranged under Clement XIII (1768) who had the fishpond beyond the Loggia of the Casina enlarged. He surrounded the square with little obelisks and created the access by way of a double stairway.

From this point it is possible to see the facade of the Loggia of the Casina with the inscription by Pius IV and the one by Leo XII that mentions the restorations executed in 1824.

At that time four stucco caryatids were removed from the niches where the present statues and mosaic candleholders are. Nearby is the large statue of Cybele

115-121. *The Casina of Pius IV: the two facades on the Loggia (116 and 118), the facade and the interior of the Villa (117 and 121) and the two facades of the Science Academy.*

122

12.

124

that has graced the central niche since the Renaissance. In the spring one can see Arum Lilies (*Zantedeschia*) blooming by the fountain. The Casina of Pius IV is reached by two paths flanked by Laurel and is surrounded by a group of splendid conifers that are some of the oldest and most valuable in the gardens: ancient Cedars, Pines, Yew trees (*Taxus baccata*). A notable example of this species is the *Prunus cerasifera pissardii*, its wine-red leaves pruned into a heart shape, while the majestic Horse Chestnut (*Aesculus hippocastanum*), Mimosas, and even Bamboo hedges (*Phyllostachis aurea*), becoming golden in the summer, give a different look to this part of the gardens. Noteworthy also for the rich color in their blossoming season are large Hydrangea bushes.

The Fountain of the Mirrors is close to the new staircase built by Paul V in the new building he added to the Vatican Palaces, and which leads to the avenue called Stradone ai Giardini through an arch.

This fountain is shaped like a grotto encrusted with mosaics, and remained unfinished when Pope Paul died in 1621. At the base of the columns is the Borghese coat of arms.

The Fountain of the Towers is also called the Fountain of the Sacrament because the central part and lateral spouts suggest the idea of an altar with candles on either side of the Holy Sacrament. An inscription dates the fountain at 1609; its execution can possibly be attributed to Jan van Xanten and Martino Ferrabosco.

On either side of Viale dell'Aquilone are hedges of Laurel (*Laurus nobilis*) and rows of Magnolias behind them. In the background is the Fontana dell'Aquilone.

In the big square there is a large Roman terracotta jar, like those formerly used to store grain.

Begun as the "Secret Garden" under Paul III (1534-1549), the present Square Garden was endowed with the beautiful gate by Sansovino at the time of Pius IV (1559-1565).

In 1676 it was enlarged and given the name of "Square Garden." Complex restoration work was also carried out under Gregory XVI (1831-1846) who placed in its center the fountain formerly in the Courtyard of the Pigna and added 224 pots of citrus trees and his coat of arms in flowering plants.

Beyond the Pinacoteca are large pots of Azaleas, and on the surrounding outside wall a splendid Jasmine (*Jasminum*) and a *Campis radicans*, a liana of the Bignoniaceae family with beautiful orange flowers when in bloom.

On the avenue bordering the Square Garden is a variety of shrub species: *Viburnum cotoneaster, Ligustrum, Pittosporum, Juniperus, Berberis, Laurus*.

The new building of the Vatican Pinacoteca was inaugurated on 27 October 1932; it was designed by Luca Beltrami (Milan 1854-Rome 1932), and is an eclectic work inspired by Renaissance architecture. Constructed entirely of brick, it is decorated with ancient statuary, colored majolica, and mosaics.

The museum occupies part of the Renaissance Secret Garden, now called Square Garden, which was changed radically by this addition.

The Pinacoteca and the Pauline Museum behind it

125

122. *Conifer trees in the Vatican Gardens.*

123. *An avenue in the Vatican Gardens, and the bus that connects St. Peter's Square with the Vatican Museums.*

124. *The Self-service restaurant in the Vatican Museums, overlooking the Gardens.*

125. *The Fountain of the Galley.*

are examples of two different ways of creating a harmonious addition to the complex of the Vatican Palaces.

Gregory XVI built the new monumental entrance (1834) onto the Stradone ai Giardini, which was later replaced by the modern iron gate. In the inscription above, now barely visible, there are words of praise for the pope and for his restoration of the Gardens.

The Pauline Museum was built between 1966 and 1970 after plans by the architects Vincenzo, Fausto, and Lucio Passarelli. It houses, in a modern and systematic exhibition, works that were formerly located in the three museums of the Lateran which John XXIII transferred to the Vatican in 1965: the Gregorian Profane Museum, the Pio-Christian Museum and the Missionary-Ethnological Museum.

The mosaic of the athletes of the Caracalla Baths has been reconstructed in a large exedra visible from outside, and the series of arched openings under the roof (one of the most notable decorative elements looking towards the Courtyard of the Zitella, between the new museum and the Pinacoteca) allows the light to stream inside, illuminating the sculptures very effectively.

The Fontana della Zitella (Fountain of the Spinster), fed by the aqueduct of San Damaso, is adorned with a statue of a draped woman, known as "the Spinster" or as "Lucretia."

In the Gallinaro Tower, built during the time of Innocent VIII (1484-1492) simultaneously with his Palazzetto, poultry was raised for use in the Papal Palace.

Today the tower is in the center of a complex of greenhouses used by the administrators of the Gardens to grow the plants and flowers needed to beautify the Vatican Gardens and decorate the Papal Palaces.

The Pio-Clementine Museum was begun in 1771, adapting Innocent's Palazzetto, on plans by Alessandro Dori, and was continued by Michelangelo Simonetti who added the new rooms and the Sala Rotonda

126. The Fontana delle Cascatelle.

127. The Fontana della Zitella; in the background, Torre del Gallinaro overlooking the greenhouses.

128. An Orchid cultivated in the greenhouses.

129. An Acanthus in the English Garden.

130. An Anthurium cultivated in the greenhouses.

crowned with statues. It was completed by Giuseppe Camporese who designed the Atrium of the Four Gates (1786) with the overhanging Sala Rotonda, conceived as a small temple on a central plan in Palladian style.

The Palazzetto of Innocent VIII, or Innocent's Casino, constructed on Belvedere hill where the *Viridaria* gate once stood, was the first of the popes' residences for retreat erected adjacent to the Vatican Palace, and connected to it by Bramante's Stradone.

The architecture, in the form of a crenellated castle, was designed by Antonio Pollaiuolo, and constructed by Giacomo da Pietrasanta (1487), according to Vasari.

In the courtyard was the famous Gallery of the Statues instituted by Julius II in the early sixteenth century.

It was drastically altered inside and out in the second half of the eighteenth century, first by Alessandro Dori, and then by Michelangelo Simonetti to house the Pio-Clementine Museum; the second floor houses part of the Gregorian Etruscan Museum.

128

129

130

Next to the east facade of the Palazzetto, built as a separate entrance, is the famous Spiral Staircase designed by Bramante.

This brick-paved staircase is 2.32 meters wide. A horse can climb up it, as it has an incline of 17 degrees. The staircase has 36 granite columns with Doric, Ionic, and Corinthian capitals.

Begun in 1512, it was continued by Baldassarre Peruzzi under Paul III and was finished toward 1564 by Pirro Ligorio.

The Fountain of the Galley was built by Jan van Xanten and Martino Ferrabosco in 1620-21 over the fishpond of Julius III (1550-1555), next to the great supporting wall of Bramante's Stradone connecting the Vatican Palace with the Palazzetto of Innocent VIII. Van Xanten designed the imaginative galley made of lead that spurts water through its cannons; Ferrabosco was responsible for the architectural design.

The fountain was restored by Clement IX (1667-1669) and then given its present form by Pius VI (1779).

Near the fountain are some luxuriant Alocasias, with large green leaves, typical of equatorial climates. Papyrus (*Cyperus alternifolius*), a marshy plant originally from Madagascar, also grows here.

The Gardener's House includes a medieval tower that was probably part of a fortified wall that surrounded the entire palace at the time of Innocent II (1198-1216).

On the exterior of the house are the reliefs that decorated the base of the Column of the First Vatican Ecumenical Council.

Near the Gardener's House are the ruins of a wall built as defense against Saracen raids of the Vatican Basilica and the village built by Leo IV (847-855). These walls belong to the first phase of construction, unlike those already encountered that belonged to the fifteenth-century restoration of the walls.

The ancient building of the Zecca (the Mint), built by Alexander VII in 1655, was once equipped with a minting machine, invented by Bernini, that worked by water. The building was completely restored by Pius VI in 1776.

The Piazza del Forno has a seventeenth-century fountain in the center. The wing that Paul V built to connect the Palace with the Gardens (1607-8), with access to the Stradone ai Giardini through an arch, opens onto this square. Also in this square are: the beginning of the West Corridor with Torre Pia (Pius V, 1566-1572); the Sentinella gate where one enters the Cortile della Sentinella (Courtyard of the Sentry) and the Vatican Palace; the building that contains the Sistine Chapel, and finally a gate dating from the time of Urban VIII, leading to Via delle Fondamenta.